Kathi —

Forrest and Todd will forever be a part of the best of us.

Love,
Ruth

The Art of Our Healing is a must read for everyone as we all will experience the loss of a loved one. Through poetry, art, personal stories and scripture Jill and Vicky gently guide us on a journey to the heart of our Father and His healing touch.

MIKE CHAPLINSKY
Executive Director Suncoast Youth for Christ

Grief and loss are real and hard to talk about. In their heartfelt and beautifully illustrated new book, *The Art of Our Healing*, authors Vicky DeMaio and Jill Zientek wrestle with the hard questions, the doubts and fears, and the nitty-gritty issues of grief, loss, and mourning. Through real-life stories and biblical advice, anyone mired in the trenches of loss will find Godly counsel and direction as they read. They have walked the path and know it well; their experiences will guide you and give you hope.

KATE BATTISTELLI
Author *The God Dare and Growing Great Kids*

Knowing what my dear friend, Vicky, has had to endure in her life, then reading about it has given me new appreciation for God and healing as I watched how someone I know grew through all of this.. The book is a "how to" in some respects as you try to navigate through the grief process from the loss of a loved one. Having experienced two very recent losses myself, this book has helped give me the reassurance that God always has something better. We just have to open our eyes and our hearts. If you have experienced any loss in your lifetime, I would highly suggest spending some time with this book. You'll be better for it, for sure.

JOHN SHOMBY
Owner/CEO, Country's Radio Coach, Inc.

THE *Art* OF OUR HEALING

Vicky DeMaio and Jill Zientek

Carpenter's Son Publishing

The Art of Our Healing: Faith-Based Journey of Loss, Hope, and Healing,
Accompanied by Original Artwork

Published by Carpenter's Son Publishing, Franklin, Tennessee

Published in association with Shane Crabtree of Christian Book Services, LLC
www.christianbookservices.com

Scripture is used from the New King James Version, © 1982 by Thomas Nelson, Inc.
All rights reserved. Used by permission.

Scriptures marked KJV are taken from the KING JAMES VERSION (KJV): public domain.

Front Cover Art by Jill Zientek

Back Cover Art by Vicky DeMaio

Cover and Interior Design by Suzanne Lawing

Edited by Bob Irvin

Printed in the United States of America

978-1-954437-52-4

Dedications

In memory of my son, and late husband, who loved passionately, gave generously, and are with Jesus walking streets of gold. Thank you to my loving husband, family, and friends, for whose support I am forever grateful.

For all those who have lost loved ones and are hurting, this is for you. May you know His great love for you. He is but a breath away.

Vicky

I dedicate this book to my husband, Ted Zientek, the love of my life. Our love was truly a gift from God, and I am thankful for having known the love of such a kind, gentle, special man. I'll be seeing you, babe.

Love, Jill

Special "thank you"

To all those who have prayed over

"THE ART OF OUR HEALING"

when it was but a title, hope and a dream.

Thank you to......

Carpenter's Son Publishing for taking

us on this journey of bringing

"THE ART OF OUR HEALING"

to life.

We pray everyone who reads this book

will be forever changed, blessed,

and their "brokenness" healed.

Vicky and Jill

Contents

Foreword

They say misery loves company. I don't know about that. Grief is certainly miserable, but the impact of grief is not a group experience; it's one of unique intimacy and individuality. Despite the uniqueness, those in grief often do share this: an overwhelming sense of aloneness. I met Vicky and her husband, Mark, at a membership class for the church several years ago. Jill had, by that time, been in the church for several years active with our video team and entrepreneur's group. They met at a God-ordained church, Life Group, and a new journey began, which found expression in the pages of this book. I'm excited for their journey as they magnify God in their art and share their individual stories of pain and subsequent healing. C.S. Lewis once said, "God whispers to us in our pleasures, speaks in our consciences, but shouts in our pains. It is his megaphone to rouse a deaf world." These are two followers of Jesus who have responded to the pain. They are not at all miserable, they no longer sense aloneness, and they are attempting to rouse the world. That's the art of The Healer as drawn on these two lives.

LINDELL COOLEY
Lead Pastor
Grace Church:
Nashville

I first spoke with Jill Zientek the day her husband passed away. What a terrible way to make an acquaintance. As a member of our church I was just beginning to know of her. I was concerned for her and continued to observe as she gradually made herself available to others in the time after her husband's death. I did not know of Vicky DeMaio's encounters with tragedy and grief until both Jill and Vicky presented their manuscript to me. They told me of their meeting at a church home group and how God had developed their friendship. They discovered a mutual love of art as well as shared experiences through the valley of the shadow of death. Neither Jill nor Vicky have allowed pain to define them. Nor did it break their trust in God. Nor did it make them permanently miserable. On the contrary, these pages contain both hope and beauty as they remind us that God desires to heal us: mind, body, and spirit. As a pastor, I'm proud to see these two women continue to fight the fight, contend for the faith, and invite others to find strength for the journey, as they have, in Jesus.

LARRY DAY
Executive Pastor
Grace Church:
Nashville

Snowflakes

As the snow falls,

my tears fall

in perfect harmony,

grief so heavy,

I can barely see,

fifty-seven days and counting

A life I know not of,

I will miss you, forever,

my one and only love

A poem by Jill Zientek

Painting by Jill Zientek

This sailboat painting was the first time I ever painted "peace".

Jill

ONE

Saying Goodbye to the Life We Shared

I stared at the large 16 x 20 photograph on canvas, the photo I had taken of him on a cliff overlooking Flathead Lake in Polson, Montana years before on vacation while visiting two of our dearest friends. I told him how much I loved him, that I would always love him, that I had loved him with every fiber of my being, with the depths that all my heart had to offer. I had given him my all. I told him, as I patted the left side of my heart, that I would carry his love in my heart forever, and I would treasure the love and memories we made together.

As I continued to look into those beautiful blue eyes I had gazed into so many times before, it was as if an epiphany hit me. I would never say goodbye to the love we shared or the memories we made or the love I still felt for him, but I must say goodbye to the tangible life we had shared together, because he was no longer here. It wasn't humanly possible for us to continue that life. I realized at that moment, no matter how difficult it was, that I had to say goodbye to that life so I could step in to the new life God had for me in the present, in the now. As painful as it was to speak those words to my beloved, it was necessary for me, and it was time. It takes courage to accept the reality that the one you loved more than life itself is gone, never coming back to this life, the life you shared together for so long, the man you had become one with, with the Lord in the center of that marriage. To face that stark truth took the healing power of my sweet Lord, the One who had been with me every step of my grief journey, and is always with me, never leaves me nor forsakes me, and cares about what I care about. He is my constant companion, the One who has healed my broken heart.

Once I accepted my new reality, I knew it was the first (new) day of the rest of my life. The change wasn't instantaneous. It has been a process, just as going through grief is a process. Some days were one step forward and two steps back. As I said, it truly takes courage to live again. Prior to my husband's extended illness and passing, I had been a productive human being, confident and capable, juggling everyday life, business, family, dreams, and hardships, just like everyone else. Even while my husband was sick and I was caring for him, I was whole because we were still one with the Lord, and I had the covering of my husband. Once he passed, I functioned through for a period of time, but once I stopped, the reality of being a widow hit me with the force of a ton of bricks. I felt like I had been sawed in two, and in a sense I had. It was only me now; my other half is in Heaven.

When that fresh grief hits, you are in shock, traumatized, lost . . . you are trying to make sense of it all. And it is amazing the situations that come out of left field.

Everyone grieves at their own pace; there is no magic formula. Family and friends will try to help you, encourage you, and at times push you when you aren't ready. You may think you are ready to clean out those closets and give things to Goodwill or other organizations. But then the emotions start pouring in like a tidal wave, and you just can't do it. Family members get frustrated because they don't understand, and you shut down because you are in fresh grief and traumatized. Be kind to yourself. Don't let others push you or force you to make decisions you're not ready to make. The common advice in many grief-related books is to not make any major decisions for at least a year, if you have that ability. It is, at least, something to seriously consider.

I found I could paint walls and cry at the same time. Therefore, I felt as though I was being productive, I supposed, that I was taking some control of my life. I desperately tried to be productive—and yet it was to no avail. One of the best things I did for myself was to start journaling my feelings and my grief, and I spent time with the Lord every morning.

Thus began the journey of grief He would take me on. Grief is a process.

— JILL ZIENTEK

Letting Go . . .

Loved you for so long,

hard to let you go,

clothes hang so neatly,

dreams I do not know,

kisses on a picture

tears on my cheeks

months have no meaning

years just repeat,

It's time to start packing up

the memories of our life

cherish the gift of love,

It's time to say goodnight . . .

A poem by Jill Zientek

Painting by Vicky DeMaio

This painting depicts the many emotions
you experience in times of great loss.

Vicky

TWO

Shattered Dreams

*L*ife has an incredible way of throwing you curveballs when you least expect it to do so. One day you can be on the mountaintop and the next day—literally—in the throes of despair. As a young girl I dreamed of finding my prince charming, riding off into the sunset, and living happily ever after.

My former years were sweet and innocent . . . and then I grew up. I was married for 17 years, and I had the perfect family with three precious children to raise, only to learn, after those 17 years of bliss, that a divorce was looming in my seemingly great life. It's not important that I share specific details (after all, no two stories are ever alike), but what Jill and I do have in common is pain beyond belief, pain that never seems to go away. How was I to live again? Who would be my support, what would people think of me, whose fault was it, really, and especially, what would my future hold now that I would be alone for the first time? And if you have children, you're not only dealing with your own grief, but the pain your children are experiencing as well. It's a heavy weight.

A constant barrage of questions seems to endlessly bombard your confused mind, self-queries that only leave you feeling numb, somewhat hopeless, and so afraid of facing life alone. Maybe you find yourself in a similar place right now. Take heart. Before I'm through you will know beyond any doubt that there is hope. He has a name, and it is Jesus.

Being a Christian through it all, I hear Jesus' still, small voice whisper these words: ***"Fear not, for I am with you, I will uphold you with my righteous right hand"*** (Isaiah 41:10). Two years after my divorce I finally got in a routine of feeling like life could be somewhat normal again. I was introduced to a man who would later become my husband. Somehow, I was assured, he would complete the missing piece in my life. We had a wonderful marriage, and I gained two beautiful stepdaughters since his wife had passed at a young age from cancer.

We blended our family of five, and I was so glad I could breathe and live once again. We were married for 17 years, and one day it all ended abruptly due to an alcohol addiction that claimed his life.

He was gone, suddenly and unexpectedly, and again I fell into the depths of despair. A number of things can steal what is most precious to you. It is *your* story, your journey, and it is unlike anyone else's. Again, the questions began to flood my mind as I fell into self-pity on a daily basis. *Why has this happened again? How can I possibly recover from another devastating loss? I cannot muster up more courage to face another day. Why me?*

These were sad characters I had watched in movies—not things I should experience in my life. So now I had a new title: widow. The adjustment was worse than I could have imagined, even though I had great support from friends, family, and church. My world became lonely, a place set apart. *Honestly, God, how strong do you think I really am?* I want to quote the following verse in the way that makes most sense to me: ***He will never give you more than you can handle*** (1 Corinthians 10:13).

I longed for a sense of normalcy. Nothing felt right. I was a third wheel with my coupled friends, and I didn't seem to have much in common with the single widows who had been playing that role for many years. Oh, how I longed to fit in somewhere and make sense of my upside down world. Day after day life seemed to make no sense. Little did I know: God had something new on the horizon. A new chapter was about to emerge.

As I was beginning to think about wrapping up my career as a schoolteacher, I met an amazing, godly man from Franklin, Tennessee. We dated for a year before getting married. You may be thinking: I want that to happen to me. But perhaps for you it has not, and for years you have been in the same place, a widow, divorced, or waiting on some dream to be fulfilled. The big picture? None of us can ever see it, although there is One who knew us before we were born: Jesus.

"I knew you before you were born, I formed you in your mother's womb;
you are fearfully and wonderfully made" (Jeremiah 1:5).

Each of our journeys remains so unique, filled with twists and turns along a bumpy road no one would ever expect. *The important thing is to know you really have never been alone.* I was beginning to feel like Job, if you remember his story, from the Bible. Job was a righteous man who loved God, yet everything was taken from him. Thankfully, I did know the ending of his story. It was one of promise from God, one of rewarding Job for his faithfulness. Could this be my story someday? Ever wonder how your story will end? This is a question we all ponder at different times.

After dating and getting to know this man I was to marry, doing so required a great deal of changing gears, so to speak, as he lived in Tennessee. I had lived in several different cities across my thirty years in Florida. *What was on the horizon?*, I wondered. Even God asked Abraham to pack up and move.

"Get out of your country, from your family, and from your father's house, to a
land that I will show you; I will make you a great nation; I will bless you and
make your name great; and you shall be a blessing" (Genesis 12:1, 2).

People I knew kept saying to me: "The third time's a charm, Vicky. You will see." I never really believed this to be true. Honestly, I had only hoped to be married once and then live happily ever after, remember? I could hear the distant chatter from those who would never move away from what they were accustomed to; it would require too much of them. Don't we all have a fear of change and the unknown? But at this point in my life I was just grateful I had new beginnings. My soul longed for change in a dry and weary land. But deep inside, I also found myself wondering when the next shoe would drop. And from my inner circle, and even friends from afar, I was constantly being asked how I was managing my new life since I was soon to leave my son, two precious stepdaughters, church, friends, and teaching career to embark on this new adventure. Certainly, I had days I wondered if I was doing the right thing, and I needed to be sure this was God's leading.

"This is the way, walk in it" (Isaiah 30:21).

"Trust in the Lord with all your heart, and lean not on your own understanding" (Proverbs 3:5, 6).

Grieving, loss, pain, and heartache are never what any of us want to endure, but they have led me to say: *It is well with my soul.* I have learned to rest and rely on my Lord and Savior Jesus Christ. **"And the peace of God, which surpasses all understanding, will guard your hearts and minds through Christ Jesus"** (Philippians 4:7).

Two years into my new marriage, I was finally settled, healing from the previous storms. That is when I faced the most devastating news a mother can imagine: the loss of a child. My son, 32, gone and now in Heaven. I will never know the details, nor the reason, behind his suicide. Remember, the details are not important to stress over; what we all share is that pain can seem unbearable.

Now my smiles around others were forced; no one could know the deep wounds I carried. All I really understood was I must trust a God who knows my heart and all my unanswered questions. What was His plan for me? I thought: *I cannot know it or see it or ever understand it.*

"My ways are higher than yours," He whispered to me. And, **"Weeping may last a night, but joy cometh in the morning"** (Psalm 30:5.) As I cried a bucket of tears, I said to God, out loud, "I had only one son, and now he is gone." I heard the still, small voice, which is the Holy Spirit inside me, say: "Vicky, my precious daughter, I lost my only son, Jesus." Jesus hung on a cross to save mankind from their sins and restore man to Himself to live eternally with Him just like before the fall. This was the ultimate sacrifice because of His great love for us.

"We love, because He first loved us" (1 John 4:19).

"He was beaten and wounded for our transgressions" (Isaiah 53:5).

All I needed was hope for the future and to believe His Word that tells me He will give me beauty for ashes (see Isaiah 61:3). He is a promise keeper! He will somehow restore what the locust eats away. He will give me double for my trouble, and he reminded me there will be trials and troubles in this world. James 1:2-5 states: *"My brethren, count it all joy when you fall into various trials, knowing that the testing of your faith produces patience, but let patience have its perfect work, that you may be perfect and complete, lacking nothing."*

"But take heart, for I have overcome the world" (John 16:33).

Still, I cried out: "I am human, God! I only feel sorrow and pain. *Help me!"*

"Even though I walk through the valley of the shadow of death,I will fear no evil; for You are with me; Your rod and Your staff, they comfort me" (Psalm 23:4).

This verse shows me I am walking and moving forward through my pain, but we also must recognize walking is a *forward* motion. Jesus showed me the key to being an overcomer is understanding this one Scripture: *"They overcame by the blood of the lamb and by the word of their testimony."* This was the key: my testimony. Now what do you want me to do, God, with these shattered dreams? Our deepest pain and suffering is not for ourselves alone, but to help others. Our pain is to be used to help others know they can get through any adversity with Christ. Jesus alone is the healer of my broken heart.

"He is close to the brokenhearted, and saves those crushed in spirit"
(Psalm 34:18).

"Blessed be the God and Father of our Lord Jesus Christ, the Father of mercies and God of all comfort, who comforts us in all our tribulation, that we may be able to comfort those who are in any trouble with the comfort with which we ourselves are comforted by God" (2 Corinthians 1:3-5).

Now I am sharing my testimony, counseling, and leading a Bible study while offering my experiences to help others fulfill their destiny. Could it be that your shattered dreams will turn into your greatest blessings? Could it be . . .

— Vicky DeMaio

Painting by Jill Zientek

I especially related to the eyes and the expression
on the cat's face during the early days of my grief.

Jill

THREE

The Widow's Brain

Yes, there is such a thing as a widow's brain. My family doctor told me that the chemistry in our brains changes with the trauma of loss. The knowledge of that truth was freeing because I knew I was not myself and not thinking correctly. I was not able to handle stressful situations as I once had. There were times I just needed to go lie down somewhere! Some days I couldn't accomplish anything. Some days I might be able to accomplish one thing. And on those special occasions when I felt like I was really coming back, I was elated . . . but it wouldn't last, and I felt like I was back to square one again. Again, grief is very much a process, and it can be debilitating at times, as well as traumatizing, and can affect your brain and ability to function at a normal level. At least, that was my experience.

I remember having my elderly mother write checks for me to pay my bills as I stood behind her and cried. I was totally devastated, and I was struggling to do everyday tasks that were once so simple and easy to complete. I struggled to make decisions of any kind and became easily overwhelmed.

By the grace of God and the passing of time, I have become myself again, and I now feel confident in making decisions, writing checks, paying bills, all the things that go with the running of a home. So don't beat up on yourself if you too have struggles to complete simple, everyday tasks. This is a process. It takes time to find your new normal. With God's help, all things are possible.

I can do all things through Christ which strengtheneth me.
Philippians 4:13, KJV

Wait on the Lord: be of good courage, and He shall strengthen thine heart; wait, I say, on the Lord. Psalm 27:14, KJV

Photography by Jill Zientek

The ominousness of this barn lent itself to the idea
and title of this chapter "The Wolves are Coming."

Jill

FOUR

The Wolves Are Coming

*I*n those first, few, fresh days of grief, you are so fragile, vulnerable, and literally in shock. For some, the whole world just came crashing down, and they can barely make it through the day. If you are one of the lucky ones, family and friends will call quite frequently to check on you, but after they discover they have no answers—and, quite frankly, just can't take the heaviness of your grief any longer—you will stop hearing from them. It's hurtful and painful, but necessary, as they are not equipped to bear the heaviness of your grief. Only God, Jesus, and the Holy Spirit can bear that load. The sooner you realize this truth, the sooner your journey of grieving and healing will truly begin.

This chapter's title is a reference to those who do not have your best interests at heart. Wolves come in all different sizes and with plenty of different kinds of agendas. One could be a repairman charging too much for his services, just because he knows you are a widow. *Greed* is a nasty wolf that seems to show up in so many situations. *Jealousy* and *bitterness* are two wolves that seem to prowl a great deal when a widow is down on her luck. True colors always seem to come to light.

 The coldness of people coming into a widow's home and laying claim to possessions before her husband's body is even laid in the ground is truly unbelievable. If a widow and her husband's wills and legal documents are not in proper order, she may be in danger of being evicted from her home, the home she shared with her husband just days before his death.

Some widows will be aggressed by improper suitors. Seriously, the last thing on her mind is an improper fling. A large percentage of widows will lose their homes as they have no way of paying the debt that is owed on the home and no employment to support the debt, as they might have been their husband's caregiver. She may be entitled to widow's benefits, but that is only a small portion of the funds she will need to secure her financial future. No wonder our Lord made special provisions for widows and orphans. He knew the struggles those in these two life situations would endure.

Thankfully, our Lord is a way maker, and upon the death of her husband, the Lord becomes the widow's husband. He is her protector, her provider, her defender. He is her everything. Trust in the Lord with all your heart . . . all ye widows.

— Jill Zientek

Keep the Scriptures that follow before your eyes and on your lips daily. The word of the Lord is sharper than any two-edged sword, and the Lord is a protector of those who belong to Him.

The Lord will destroy the house of the proud;
but he will establish the border of the widow.
Proverbs 15:25, KJV

For thy Maker is thine husband; the Lord of hosts is his name;
and thy Redeemer the Holy One of Israel; The God of the
whole earth shall he be called. Isaiah 54:5, KJV

I will not leave you comfortless: I will come to you. John 14:18, KJV

He healeth the broken in heart, and bindeth up their wounds. Psalm 147:3, KJV

No weapon that is formed against thee shall prosper; and every tongue that shall rise against thee in judgment thou shalt condemn. This is the heritage of the servants of the Lord, and their righteousness is of Me saith the Lord.

Isaiah 54:17, KJV

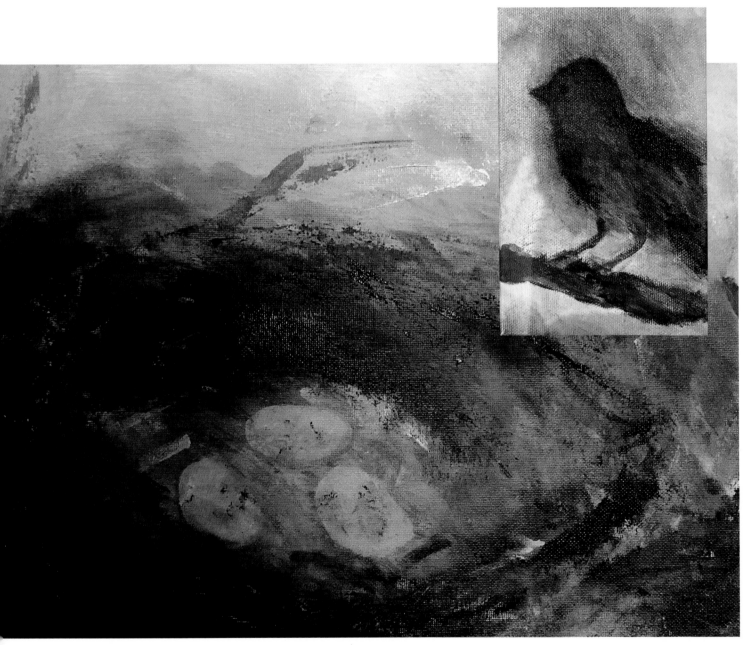

Painting by Vicky DeMaio

I love the many bird nests I see in our neighborhood on my walks. This inspired me to paint these two paintings!

Vicky

FIVE

His Eye Is on the Sparrow

*I*n our time of grief and despair, we sometimes overlook the fact that some-one greater than ourselves has full view of everything happening in our lives. I find it fascinating that God, in Scripture, would contrast an eagle and a sparrow for us to learn of His great tenderness and love. Luke 12:6, 7 tells us: ***"Are not five sparrows sold for two copper coins? And not one of them is forgotten before God."***

The Lord tells us we are of more value than many sparrows. These small birds aren't anything to write home about, and yet Jesus tells us *not a single one is forgotten by God.* He tells us we have more value than these seemingly insignif-icant birds. Now contrast the great eagle. These soaring birds are a symbol of freedom and peace; they are majestic and powerful, incredible to behold when we are able to see one up close. Back to sparrows: they symbolize creativity, productivity, and simplicity. Think about this! What a contrast; the two birds have similarities, yet they are so extremely different in purpose and strength.

Our suffering can parallel this picture. Some of our pain we can use to relate well with others; there may be similarities to our stories. But many times there exists a severe contrast in the way we handle loss and experience trauma. Some of us may be best represented by the sparrow, who suffers silently. This type of person does not want to be seen by others. But others seem to have moved past their pain and soar above it all, something like the eagle.

I live in Franklin, Tennessee where I get to experience a deep change of seasons; this is always amazing. We have a wonderful back porch where my husband and I sit for hours enjoying the wondrous outdoors. The beauty lies in the lush greenery that surrounds us on every side. Thanks to the great weather we have, we get to see the annual in full bloom for much of the year. Each day we witness sparrows, mourning doves, and robins flitting about. The neighbor who lives directly behind us has seven bird feeders in her yard. We are just several feet from those feeders and get to experience a bird show daily! The birds play about and dive-bomb the various feeders, then perch on the fence and sing to others, calling them to join the festivities, to enjoy the scrumptious seed.

I've been able to watch their every move on many occasions. Something I discover is that there does not appear to be one sick bird among them. They eat to their heart's content without a care in the world. They seem to have a language to themselves as they chirp and sing to one another all day long.

These are truly fascinating birds that seem to have one objective: finding food and community. Seldom do I see one sparrow acting alone. Sparrows are small birds, ranging from 4 to 6 inches in length, living in wooded areas, typically staying low to the ground, and flying at fast speeds. They are found in every continent of the world except the Far East and Antarctica.

In comparison, eagles are much larger, majestic birds with distinct features, a wingspan of 1.8 meters, and eyesight that is eight times stronger than that of humans! We often find them perched high upon the rocks or cliffs as we strain to look extremely high to view them. Maybe this is why the Lord tells us, in Isaiah 40:31, *"But those who wait on the Lord shall renew their strength, they shall mount up with wings like eagles. They shall run and not grow weary. They shall walk and not faint."*

I believe no matter how high or low we go in this life, the Father's eye is keenly aware of our comings and goings. He allows us to soar above life's painful experiences. He knows when we are on the mountaintop soaring like

the eagle or hidden in the vast array of the dense forest where no one can find us. When darkness falls, we sometimes cannot see our way out, but we can rest assured Jesus will shine His light, illuminating our path as we struggle to make sense of our losses.

> *"Look at the birds of the air, for they neither sow nor reap nor gather into barns, yet your heavenly Father feeds them and cares for them. Are <u>you</u> not of more value then they?"* (Matthew 6:26, emphasis mine).

When we have lost someone who is so precious to us, it is hard to gain any perspective other than our loss. It becomes our single focus, and if we are not careful it will consume us. Our life becomes introspective, and we lose sight of the eagle's perspective, which is that bird's-eye view, but more important-ly, of God's view or perspective, which is simple: His ways are higher than our ways.

Oh, my friend, we have much to live for, as this life is fleeting. And we must know He designed a better life for us from the beginning of time. Shall we dare crack the door to His glorious light and allow Him to heal our broken places and, in doing so, restore our souls?

May I dare ask which you are: the sparrow or the eagle? One that soars at extreme heights while seeing the world from many different perspectives? Or are you more like the sparrow, who flits from one place to the next in the shadows, staying close to what's familiar and away from any prey that can devour?

Neither place is right or wrong, but our perspective is what will make or break us. Again, we see God using the sparrow to teach us a lesson of humility and utter trust. He lets us know how valuable we are to Him. Surely, we can glean much from these birds, contrasting them to our fragile lives here on earth. The stage is set for something much greater than the eye can see. It's apparent He wants us to soar above our grief and pain, knowing something greater is about to unfold in our lives.

It's in the faint chirp of the sparrow that we hear Him calling out to us to draw near and place our broken heart in His hands. He loves to tell me, "Do not be afraid. I am holding you in the palm of My hand." A hand that holds only those who belong to Him. He shoulders all our burdens and asks us to cast our cares upon Him. Isn't it comforting to know? Yes, His eye is still on the sparrow.

— Vicky DeMaio

Painting by Jill Zientek

This painting was very passionate, physical and emotional.
It poured out of me like a raging river.

Jill

SIX

Forgiveness

Forgiveness sounds easy. In theory. But where the flesh, pride, and heart are concerned, it gets a little tricky.

God calls us to forgive one another so He can forgive us. Forgiveness is non-negotiable. The longer we hold out forgiving others, the longer we endure the pain of our transgression. Our minds are consumed by the offense, haunted by the details. Sometimes the unforgiveness turns into out "right": hatred toward the person, or persons, involved. It is poison to us, as surely as if we drank a fatal potion from a glass. And it robs us of our peace, that peace that passes all understanding, the peace only God can give to those who belong to him.

The painting that accompanies this chapter is called "Forgiveness." The work is a 3-foot by 3-foot canvas I labored over trying to work out a situation. At the time, I did not know I was painting about forgiveness, but I was painting with physical passion as I slapped the colors on the canvas. I was painting with aggression. I didn't particularly like what I was painting, and I was totally unaware the Holy Spirit was drawing me. If you look at the upper right hand corner of the painting, you will see the Holy Spirit drawing me. As you look to the center of the painting my heart is churning with unforgiveness, even outright anger. It was a process that took several days, but finally, with a friend's keen eye and intuitive, Godly Spirit, I came to know that this painting was about my need to forgive in a situation—and that's exactly what I did with the Holy Spirit's help and guidance. My peace returned and, to this day, I have only a vague recollection of the details of the situation.

When we forgive, God makes a work in our hearts, in our minds. His love for us is absolutely beautiful, and He really does know what is best for us.

We all have free will. God won't make you forgive, but you will be miserable if you don't.

One more thing: just because you forgive someone doesn't mean you will have reconciliation. However, you are still called to forgive with your entire heart. It is this process that will set you free of the situation, and you will be pleasing to your Father in Heaven. This allows Him to make a complete work in all hearts concerned.

— Jill Zientek

And when ye stand praying, forgive, if ye have ought against any: that your Father also which is in heaven may forgive you your trespasses. Mark 11:25, KJV

If we confess our sins, He is faithful and just to forgive us our sins, and to cleanse us from all unrighteousness. 1 John 1:9, KJV

Painting by Jill Zientek

My goldendoodle Stella was my muse' for this painting.
I had a lot of fun painting this piece of art!

Jill

SEVEN

What Is Your Pickleball?

*I*t's been three and half years since my husband left this world. In the beginning of my fresh grief phase, I was devastated by my beloved's passing. He was my everything, the other half of me. When he went to Heaven, my passion went with him. I just didn't care anymore—about anything. I functioned through, which is what I had to do.

I remember being in a class, early on, trying to reinvent myself, as I was too young to be a widow and needed to find a way to work to support myself. The bubbly young lady at the front of the class told us to write down a vacation goal to motivate ourselves to success. I had nothing. No desire whatsoever. I felt like crying.

As the months went by, I found doing things with others that I had not done with my beloved put some "normal" back into my life—a new normal, of sorts. But it wouldn't last. I would think I was gaining ground but would find it to no avail. Whatever the newfound experience, it was only temporary, and my constant companion, grief, returned front and center. Thankfully, my sweet Lord was by my side, and He never left me during my journey of grief.

I tried to muscle through my grief at different times, but again, this was with no success. The healthy journey of grieving would be in God's timing, not mine.

Everyone grieves differently, so don't let anyone dictate to you how you should grieve or not grieve. Grief is a personal journey. I felt it was the most painful and wonderful journey of my life. Painful in the loss of my sweet love from this world—the tangible part of him and our love together here on earth. Wonderful in the way the Lord held me so tightly the first morning I woke up without my sweet husband. God cared so deeply and completely about me.

I will not leave you comfortless: I will come to you. John 14:18, KJV

He healeth the broken in heart, and bindeth up their wounds. Psalm 147:3, KJV

So you have to ask yourself: *What is this? What is my pickleball?* For me, it was when I got my passion for something to return. I truly loved to play pickleball, the tennis-like game played on a smaller court. But I was terrified to plug myself into something so social all by myself. On the drive over to play for the first time, I was thinking, *Why am I doing this? I should just go back home.* It took all the courage I had just to get out of the car and go in.

But once I started playing, hitting the ball, I was alive again! The Lord had given joy and passion back to me through a game I once loved to play. "The joy of the Lord is my strength." So . . . find your pickleball. It might be painting, dancing, learning to play piano or guitar, traveling, or learning a foreign language. Ask the Lord to help you find your joy and passion again; He *will* help you. The Lord is good and He is faithful, and He cares deeply about you. The joy of the Lord is your strength. So I challenge you to challenge yourself: step out and do something you have never done before and see how it makes you feel. You are alive, and God has a good and perfect plan for your life. Go find your pickleball.

— Jill Zientek

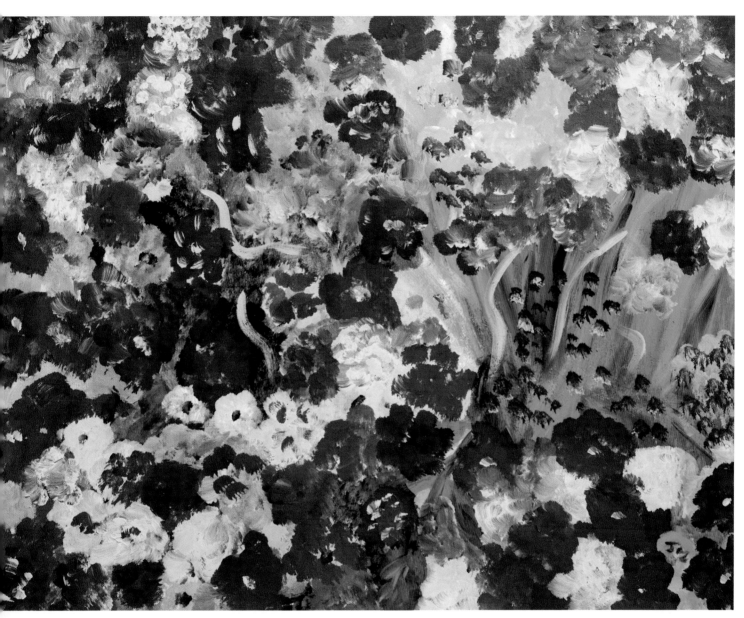

Painting by Jill Zientek

The name of this painting is Joyous Explosion. It reminds me of an ocean of flowers. The brilliance and happiness of this painting made it the perfect choice for the "Thankful" chapter.

Jill

EIGHT

Thankful

I remember waking up the first morning after my beloved had died. God was holding me so tight. His arms were around me on every side, as if I were in a barrel. I could be nothing but thankful. Thankful for the beautiful life we had shared, thankful for the love we had given each other completely and with sur-render, and thankful that he was no longer in pain and suffering, but now with our Lord in Heaven forever. I was thankful that I knew, within my heart, that I would see him again, that this was only a temporary separation. I have told friends and loved ones and acquaintances: if I had not known, without a shadow of doubt, that I would see my beloved again, no one could have consoled me. Our love was real. It was deep. It was passionate. And my loss has been mighty and life-shattering, but because of the love of my Father in Heaven, my sweet Jesus, and my precious Holy Spirit, my broken heart has been healed, mended, repaired.

You may be wondering: how in the world could she be thankful after losing a love that strong, that all-encompassing? Actually, it is because of that love. God is love, and His love was at the center of the love between my beloved and myself.

God knew that we would have deep sorrow, even as others do who have no hope. But we put our hope in Jesus Christ, and we know He is coming back on a white horse to gather all who belong to Him. We live in a fallen world, and even as good as it can be much of the time, it is only a temporary home. Our time on earth is like a vapor on the water. Our permanent home is Heaven.

So I would say to all of you who are grieving the loss of a spouse, a child, a marriage, a sibling, grandparents, or a friend who sticks closer than a brother— whomever is so deeply important in your life, but now is gone—be thankful for having known that person, for having experienced the kind of love and warmth that is truly a gift from God.

And always remember: God can work with a thankful heart.

— Jill Zientek

But I would not have you to be ignorant, brethren, concerning them which are asleep, that ye sorrow not, even as others which have no hope.

For if we believe that Jesus died and rose again, even so them also which sleep in Jesus will God bring with Him.

For this we say unto you by the word of the Lord, that we which are alive and remain unto the coming of the Lord shall not prevent them which are asleep.

For the Lord himself shall descend from heaven with a shout, with the voice of the archangel, and with the trump of God: and the dead in Christ shall rise first.

Then we which are alive and remain shall be caught up together with them in the clouds, to meet the Lord in the air: and so shall we ever be with the Lord.

Wherefore comfort one another with these words. 1 Thessalonians 4:13-18, KJV

Oh So Lovely

There is something about silence,

Oh, so lovely,

memories, tenderly and

gently nudge me,

A heart content with its fate,

whispers of tomorrow

anxiously await,

territory in my heart

that belongs only to you,

flowers blossom

with love all anew

A poem by Jill Zientek

Painting by Vicky DeMaio

My focus here was to paint the beauty creation has to offer us every day. Just as a sunset has an array of colors, so can grief manifest itself in similar ways.

Vicky

NINE

Don't Let Grief Define You

At times when we have passed through the dark places in our lives, or are in the midst of them, we don't realize that our grief has caused us, in essence, to stand still in time. We are frozen in a state of despair, and nothing around us seems to matter like it used to. People, places, and everyday life seem to have little or no meaning. Grief is a mental and emotional state that causes distress and pain and usually refers to sorrow or the loss of someone or something.

In other words, grief is the natural reaction to loss. Some examples of life changes that bring grief can be leaving home, an extended illness, death of a spouse or loved one, change of job, loss of financial security, and many more. One thing we can take away from these types of losses is that we have no choice but to find a new way to navigate life from a different perspective. Life will go on whether you choose to move with it or not. Grief can be a constant state of emotional trauma for an extended period of time, but it was never meant to define who you are. God told us that we would have trouble in this life. Did Jesus grieve? Of course He did. We see Him weeping and grieving with others in the Bible. Jesus is well acquainted with this powerful emotion. ***"Weeping may last but a night, but joy cometh in the morning"*** (Psalm 30:5).

Why did God say "joy comes in the morning"? I believe it's because, when we have been in a hard place, He wants us to understand we don't need to stay there long. Our future holds something better even when we can't see it or feel it. God wants us to live an abundant life, and we can't live an abundant life if we are forever grieving.

Hold dear the memories you have that are wonderful memories, the ones that cause you to be thankful for the time spent with the loved one. ***"Finally, brethren, whatsoever things are true, whatsoever things are pure, whatsoever things are just, whatsoever things are of a good report, if there is any virtue and if there is anything praiseworthy, meditate on these things"*** (Philippians 4:8). Here we see it is actually a choice, a mindset. I can choose joy and peace even in the midst of the worst difficulties.

Life is fleeting on earth. Let's be sure we don't miss out on all the wonder around us. One of the most powerful anecdotes to missing out is thankfulness. What are you thankful for today? After losing a spouse, a son, and my parents, I can say I am thankful for many more things than I deserve. I am thankful for my new husband, my children, my grandkids, my church, my home, my friends, my health, and much, much more.

Our choices determine our destiny. Every day is a gift, and most of us know, if we have suffered loss of any kind, that loss brings this into sharper focus. Grab all the support you can, love with all your heart, accept those things that are out of your control, and forgive those who offend you. Jesus tells us that He sticks closer than a brother. Isn't it wonderful to know that even if I don't have anyone to talk with, He is there at any time and is the best listener I could possibly have? He is the same yesterday, today, and forever. Oh, how this makes me feel wonderful!

So, my friend, what defines you? Are you defined by what has happened to you? I run into people who are defined by their grief. Their conversations always seem to revert back to pain and lack of acceptance regarding their tough circumstances. Think seriously about why God tells us that "as a man thinketh, so is he." Sobering, isn't it?

We need a new mindset that includes thinking about our purpose and His plan for our lives. Your grief and pain can be a starting point for helping others get through their tough times. Helping others is such good therapy; it helps us heal much more quickly. Today is a new day! Embrace it, celebrate it, know you are never alone.

Nights may seem long, and the curtains may be drawn, but this is not your final chapter.

— Vicky DeMaio

Painting by Vicky DeMaio

This painting is one of my favorites. Seasons bring change and change is necessary to hope for something new.

Vicky

TEN

Seasons Come and Seasons Go

*E*cclesiastes 3:1-4: *"To everything there is a season, a time for every purpose under heaven: A time to be born, a time to die, a time to plant, and a time to pluck what is planted. A time to weep, and a time to laugh; a time to mourn and a time to dance."*

I love seasons! In Florida, where I lived for 30 years, you don't really experience true seasons. The climate simply goes from hot to hotter to hottest! OK, that is a bit of a stretch. There really are some delightful months of cool weather before having to duck into the air conditioning for the rest of the year.

Moving to Tennessee has greatly helped me appreciate the seasons. We really do have a spring, summer, fall, and winter. They are all so distinctly different in so many ways. I grew up in Michigan where the winter seasons were long and dreary and seemed like they would never end. I correlate that harsh season to months of grief and sadness. My recollection of many of those days were long periods of dark, cold, and gray. There was not much to look forward to since the temperatures could drop to minus 10, or below, on any given day! I couldn't wait for spring to finally appear, the ice to start melting, and to begin packing up my sweaters, wool coat, and mittens. It meant freedom to be outdoors again, to reunite with old friends, to plan long, needed summer vacations.

Have you noticed that every season is different from the last, that there is always something new to look forward to, especially the distinct scents and smells of spring? Flowers are in full bloom, and the trees are beginning to bud with magnificent colors. As a child I remember my mother couldn't wait to take me to the farmers market each week to pick out fresh corn, pole beans, and delicious watermelon. Somehow each season brings a longing for something new, the anticipation that change is in the air.

When you have experienced loss, a change of season can become fearful and dreadful to say the least. It's as if you can't move one step forward; you are stuck in your circumstances, immobilized. Days, months, and even years seem to blend together as life becomes a blur. Life around you seems to stand still while you find your emotional state has become numb to what is happening around you. The beauty in everyday living has been taken away as you continue to drown in a pool of self-pity and grief, and your personal change of season becomes an unending season of heartache. Sadly, for many of us, this becomes our new normal.

Are you there now? Accustomed to this season year after year? I began to think about how I would work through all these emotions and grief. Do I read the grief books everyone suggests, find a support group, or find the nearest therapist? For you it may be none, one, or all of the above that you choose. But a baby step is better than no step.

What's important is you need to start by doing something. With God's help your heart will instruct you on what may be best in whatever season you find yourself. Could it be that healing in your inner person is what you really need most? The question that continued to confront me was this: who will help me sort out my frayed emotions and the enormous tasks ahead? Everyone had their own life; they seemed too busy to be consumed with mine. My answer, again, was, and is, simply Jesus. He will supply all you need at just the right time. It is important to have support, so if you have no one, reach out to a local church and be honest about your needs. God tells us that He is ***"our refuge and strength, a*** *very present help in times of trouble"* (Psalm 46:1). Remember, He suffered far more pain and knows the depths of our despair.

I decided to take an art class. I had never done art in my life! I never considered myself to be the creative type, although I love color and design, so I found myself up for the challenge. This seemed like good therapy for me, a hobby I could do independently of others, one held in a quiet space without many distractions. (I had enough pain to last a lifetime, I believed, and wasn't in the mood for others seeking to instruct me in this season of my loss.) I began to really enjoy my class and those I met. After the six weeks were over, looking back, I saw I had pursued it with vigor. As I was painting, I discovered that God was going to use it for a greater purpose. *"For the plans I have for you are to prosper you, to give you a hope and a future"* (Jeremiah 29:11). Could this really be true?

What season do you find yourself in now? A continued season of mourning, or one of dancing?

My art was like a dance step, one painting at a time. One step at a time. This is how grief works. There is no set way; it's one step at a time. The important point is that our seasons should change, eventually, from sadness to gladness, from weeping to joy, from sorrow to laughter. The Lord tells us, in Isaiah 61:3, to put on a garment of praise for the spirit of heaviness. Eventually, I could focus on the blessings God had given me and continues to give me each day. I could now ask God to use my paintings for His glory; I was sharing and selling my work with others. My season of despair was beginning to lift, and I felt I was beginning to find my purpose once again.

This launched me to start a Bible study in my home, and I am now able to help others alongside my husband in pastoral counseling. Don't ever forget that God has placed inside of you talents and specific gifts He has uniquely given you. We are to discover what they are and use them.

Life is messy, but your mess can become your greatest message to others who are hurting or in need. Be purposeful to move into your new season as seasons come and go. God teaches us to press on and persevere even when the road is rough. ***"Behold, the former things have come to pass, and new things I declare, before they spring forth I tell you of them"*** (Isaiah 43:18,19). I love how God uses the words "spring forth"! Again, it's a forward motion of something unexpected to come.

Oh, how we struggle with taking one day at a time and understanding that each day is a gift. When you have experienced loss of any kind, you often become more keenly aware of your own mortality. What person can add a single hour to their life (Luke 12:25)? God instructs us to not worry about tomorrow since ***"tomorrow has enough trouble of its own"*** (Matthew 6:34). It takes discipline to not worry about tomorrow or our future. I have learned that every day is precious, and we are only promised today.

Realistically, not one of us is going to escape heartache and trials; it's what we ultimately do with them that will determine whether we move into our next season or stay stuck, year after year, in the same one.

It's time to move forward, my friend. We really have no choice. There is still much to experience and enjoy. Seasons come and go. Don't let your hard season define or rob you of the amazing future plans that await you.

— Vicky DeMaio

My Heart

My heart is heavy, who can know

The days, the hours, as they come and go

Oh help me God, not focus forever on the latter

It's trusting in You daily that will really matter.

You promise to bottle every tear

Please Lord, I need to have you here.

One day there will be no more sadness

As I awake with so much gladness.

My heart belongs to only you

Show me how you can heal it and make it new.

A poem by Vicky DeMaio

Painting by Vicky DeMaio

This painting reminds me of our journey in life. Which path shall
I take? Where you lead, I will follow.

Vicky

ELEVEN

This A-way, That A-way

*A*s a schoolteacher for many years, one of the words I heard over and over while working with students was "focus!" Kids go from one activity to another and are often so distracted by way too much stimuli that they aren't able to truly focus on the task at hand. It is our human nature to always look at what we feel is the central focus of our problem, or what we don't have, or how to attain what we don't have. Wasn't this the case with Jesus' disciples when they were in the boat and a big storm appeared, as the waves came crashing in? The disciples' only focus was on not sinking and perishing! If they only knew the Son of God was with them, the One who created the wind and waves, who could calm the seas in an instant, they might have had a bit more peace. If only we believe God is with us in every storm of life, every storm when we feel as if we are sinking from despair and there is no one to help in our life-threatening situations.

I often think of the story of Adam and Eve in the garden. God said, ***"Of every tree in the garden you may freely eat, but of the tree of the knowledge of good and evil you shall not eat, for in the day that you eat of it you shall surely die"*** (Genesis 2:16, 17). Eve focused her attention on what she thought she couldn't have, and that led to a disastrous ending. If she had gone "that a-way" instead of "this a-way," life would certainly look different for us all!

So what does all this have to do with loss, grief, and helplessness? If we continue to focus on all we have lost for long periods of time, we will never understand the true meaning of hope the way the Bible defines it. In the New Testament the Greek word for hope is *elpis*, and it means a confident expectation or anticipation of something good. That means that, even as bleak as circumstances may seem, it's not over for you. When our entire hope is in Christ, we can rest assured His promises are always for us. He will turn our situation around for our good. Roman 8:28: ***"And we know that all things work together for good to them who love God, to them who are called according to His purpose."*** God's hope never disappoints us. We can be sure of this; His word tells us so! It takes discipline to be focused, but what are we focused on day after day, year after year? Let's learn to focus on what is *eternal* and not what is *temporal*. God's desire is to help us understand that this life is fleeting and His Kingdom is forever. So if our focus is just about our pain, year after year, we will never have the proper focus on what God has planned for us on the other side of this life. Many of us miss this, unfortunately, because our mind is focused on the temporal.

Our life is made up of so many choices! I believe our choices determine our destiny. Our choices have eternal consequences. Noah, from the Old Testament, was a great example of this. People mocked him and laughed at him for building an ark when it hadn't rained in years! He stayed focused on what God told him to do, however, despite the hardships he endured day after day, month after month, year after year. He made a decision that had enormous consequences during his time as a prophet. He fulfilled his destiny and was rewarded greatly by the Lord. We too can have such an impact on the world around us if we make wise choices regarding our daily decisions despite what we are facing. Choosing to stay healthy in the midst of despair and heartache is essential. Sometimes we have so much to take care of—being a caregiver, living the life of a widow or widower, dealing with a divorce—that life can seem overwhelming.

Remind yourself to take one day at a time and not get bogged down with choices that seem insurmountable. The key to making good choices is to have peace about them while sharing those decisions, if needed, with those you trust and have your best interest at heart. ***"The Lord will guide you continually, and satisfy*** *your soul in drought, and strengthen your bones: you shall be like a watered garden, and like a spring of water, whose waters do not fail*" (Isaiah 58:11).

Over many years, I have seen how wrong choices can lead one down dark paths of anxiety, fear, and self-destruction. I love the Scripture that says, *"You will keep him in perfect peace whose mind is stayed on You, because he trusts in You"* (Isaiah 26:3). Wow, I can really have perfect peace in a tumultuous world? We are instructed to be anxious for nothing, but to focus and meditate on things that are true, noble, just, pure, lovely, and of good report.

Now, I know none of this is easy, but I have learned that if I meditate on these things it really does bring me peace! Why? Jesus is the Prince of Peace! Look to Him and let Him direct your steps. The path is never easy, but the choice to put Him first will never disappoint. How do I know this? I have lived it, experienced it, and continue to allow Jesus to be my daily focus. So my question to you is simple. What choices will you make going forward to bring you peace, long-lasting joy, and hope? Allow yourself to look at the painting that accompanies this chapter for a few minutes . . .

See yourself on this path, hand in hand with Jesus by your side. As you walk together, can you hear Him whisper your name while He speaks ever so gently . . .

Your ears shall hear a word behind you, saying "this is the way, walk in it"
(Isaiah 30:21).

Painting by Vicky DeMaio

Paint me happy! A colorful bouquet is
all I need to keep me smiling!

Vicky

TWELVE

For Such a Time as This

What an amazing God we have. How he weaves different people in and out of our lives. While attending a small life group meeting derived from Grace Church: Nashville located in Franklin, Tennessee, a lady named Jill walked into the room and sat next to me. She was bubbly and fun and I instantly took to her personality. In short, we were able to share a few things about ourselves, and the one thing we had in common was the loss of a spouse. Jill and I connected very quickly, as if we had known each other for years. Was this a divine appointment? I had met many others in social settings but something, this time, was different.

As we left the group that night we exchanged phone numbers, and later the following week, we reconnected again, this time over coffee on my back porch. We talked about our lives and our personal losses. I remember Jill asking if I had ever thought of writing a book. I said, "Never." I wasn't a writer, and I was busy counseling and enjoying my newfound hobby of painting. Jill shared that she was an artist as well.

What was God up to? Would he really put us together for such a time as this? I do believe in divine appointments, and I knew this was one of them. Our meetings led us to share the more personal details of our individual losses, and this gave us an instant bond. This was the beginning of putting our ideas together to think and pray about what could come next. We scheduled a time to share our artwork and paintings, and to begin formulating a strategy about specific chapters we would write. Soon our ideas and conversations led to putting this book together. We pray it has blessed you no matter where you are on your grief walk and journey.

He will make your crooked paths straight, and you will know He is Immanuel, "God with us." The only way Jill and I could have survived our personal tragedies is to have known Jesus. For those of you who have never heard of Him, or known Him, He is all you need to move forward and live the abundant life.

Here is a simple prayer you can pray to receive Jesus as your Lord and Savior. I promise: He will never leave you or forsake you. He is there for you always, even in the most difficult seasons of your life.

Prayer of Salvation

Lord,

I want to know who You are. I believe You are the Son of God, that You died, were buried, and rose on the third day and now sit at the right hand of the Father. I ask You to forgive me of all my sins. I recognize I cannot live this life without You. I want You to be Lord of my life. I let go of all my sinful ways and surrender all to You. I thank You, Lord, that You receive me now as your son/daughter and that I will now live my life in faith and trust I am a new creature in Christ. The old has gone and the new has come. In Jesus' majestic name I pray.

Amen

"They overcame by the blood of the Lamb and by the word of their testimony . . . " (Revelation 12:11)

— Vicky DeMaio

A Life Cut Short

No one could have prepared me for the words "Jill are you sitting down" and for the words that would follow, "Your momma is dead." All I could do was hold my head in my hands as I cried out, Oh My God, Oh My God, Oh My God over and over again. I was in shock and couldn't make sense of what I was being told. Mom had fallen victim to a home invasion. She had been robbed, murdered, her home trashed and her car stolen. This horrific, heinous event would occur on Saturday, July 23, 2022, just days before the manuscript of this book "THE ART OF OUR HEALING" was being sent to the printer to begin the process for the October 4, 2022 release.

After calling my brother Chad and telling him our mother had been killed, everything went into a tail spin, my thoughts along with it. I just wanted to run. I needed to be in motion, I needed to move. Thankfully, God had sent a close friend to be with me shortly before the news would be delivered so that I wouldn't be alone.

As I lay in bed that first night, horrible thoughts bombarding my mind,

I reached up in the dark and said, Jesus, You gotta help me, I can't do this without You! Sleep escaped me until the early dawn and I felt as if I would never sleep again. I went to church that Sunday and at the time of prayer invitation, I nearly ran to the altar and threw myself at the feet of my Savior.

One of the sweet prayer team ladies prayed over me, as if she knew my story. She prayed for sweet sleep, she prayed against fear, she prayed the truth would come out and so much more. Peace began to settle within me. As more and more saints began to pray for me I felt an overwhelming sense of peace. The outpouring of love has been humbling.

Grief has come to my door once more....

"The most exciting part of this book for mom was the page with the prayer of salvation.......she felt that page alone would help so many people to be saved and know Jesus. She prayed diligently over this book. She was a beautiful woman with a quiet and gentle spirit. A prayer warrior and an undeniable child of the most high God."

-Jill

Mary King Abrams
Born June 14, 1939, died July 23, 2022

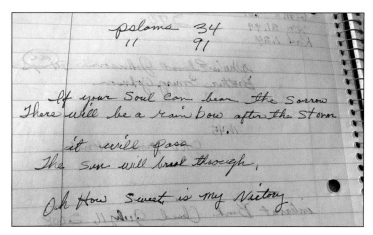

handwritten note by Mary King Abrams

Everyday Is a Gift From God

I was extremely privileged to have met Jill's mother, Mary King Abrams, a short time ago, in Jill's beautiful home in Franklin, TN. Mary was warm and inviting, and her countenance exuded the joy of the Lord. I felt I had known her my whole life. It was evident to me she was a woman of faith, who had lived her life well and to the fullest.

As we sat and talked about life and our past, we had some good laughs between us. I especially remember telling her about the time I had accepted Christ and while sharing with my dad, he interrupted me abruptly saying, "Who are you trying to be Barbara Mandrell?" Mary got the biggest kick out of that, and from then on that sealed our friendship. We talked about our book and had made plans to stay with her for three nights while Jill and I attended our first trade show in Lexington, KY. Little did we know only weeks later her life would be taken, resulting in one of the most horrific crimes imaginable.

One cannot understand such evil. I could barely begin to comprehend the grief Jill and her brother Chad were about to experience. Mary was now absent from her body and present with the Lord. "The righteous man who dies is taken from evil and enters into peace." Isaiah 57:1-2. "For me to live is Christ, and to die is gain." Philippians 1:21. I had recently heard our Pastor talk about trials and challenges in life as "tests," only to find this would be one of the biggest tests Jill and her brother would face. How could this be? We had just completed our book on grief. Faith and trusting in Jesus will carry you through even when nothing makes sense.

Both Jill and I are reminded of the scripture we used at the end of our book which rings true now more than ever. "They overcame by the blood of the Lamb and by the word of their testimony." Revelation 12:11. "We cannot do this in our own strength, when we are weak, He is strong." 2 Corinthians 12:10. Jill told me her mom used to use the phrase "Don't slop this up," meaning don't mess it up. I see Mary in heaven now, cheering us on, with this book gently laying in her hands, saying, "Girls, lives are at stake, don't slop this up!" We will see you again Mary King Abrams upon our coming Home.

-Vicky

For More from the Authors

To book Vicky and Jill for a speaking engagement, contact us at:
Vicky DeMaio: vickydemaio7@gmail.com
Jill Zientek: jillzphoto@comcast.net

Check out Vicky and Jill's Website:

www.theartofourhealing.com

Purchase books directly from Vicky and Jill's website,
and find out more about the authors!

Jill's Christmas line:
You can purchase Jill's handcrafted Christmas ornaments, Christmas
box art (sizes 6 x 6, 8 x 8, and 12 x 12), Christmas coasters and Christmas
necklaces. She also has artwork depicting historic Franklin, Tennessee.

www.jillzphoto.com

Contact Vicky DeMaio directly to purchase her paintings:
vickydemaio7@gmail.com

VICKY DEMAIO is a licensed pastoral counselor who helps clients in Franklin, Tennessee and surrounding areas. She and her husband, Mark, operate the counseling service Waymaker Ministries.

Vicky teaches a Bible study class for women and is passionate about helping others find their God-given purpose. Having lived abroad in Zurich, Switzerland and graduated high school from Hong Kong International School, she earned a degree in Special Education from Western Michigan University and a Masters in Learning Disabilities. She was awarded "Teacher of the Year" early in her career and eventually became state director of charter schools in Tallahassee, Florida.

Her love for abstract art is featured in this book, and she continues to sell her artwork locally and by commission. She has a blended family of six with four precious grandchildren. Her husband Mark is a Singer/Songwriter and Recording Artist. They reside in Franklin, Tennessee, and Vicky is a member of Grace Church–Nashville.

JILL ZIENTEK was born in Hamilton, Ohio. At the time, her parents Jack and Mary Abrams, born and raised in the hills of Kentucky, were making their way to greener pastures, to the Hoosier State, Indiana, where Jill and her brother Chad would spend their formative years. Even though Jill grew up in the Midwest, she has always told others that she is "southern fried."

Jill graduated from Union County High School in Liberty, Indiana, where she excelled in sports and art. She attended Indiana University East College in Richmond, where she studied the fundamentals of art, writing, and business.

Her professional career consists of retail banking and mortgage banking, and she now works as a real estate professional.

On June 1, 1991, Jill married the love of her life, Theodore "Ted" John Zientek Jr. They were married for twenty-six and a half years before Ted would leave this world to be with our Lord and Savior. In Greek, Theodore means "Gift from God," and Ted was truly Jill's gift from God.

In April 2014, Jill launched the Jill Zientek Christmas line which depicts historic Franklin, Nashville, and the middle Tennessee area. She cohosts the weekly "Homes and Loans Radio Show" (950 AM, WAKM) in Franklin, Tennessee.

Jill is a painter, artisan, and photographer. She also loves playing guitar and songwriting.

Jill lives in Franklin with her four-year-old Goldendoodle, Stella. Jill is a member of Grace Church–Nashville in Franklin.